WS**Kids**
WHITE STAR KIDS

The Chemistry of Disgusting Things

CONTENTS

THE SCIENTIFIC METHOD   4

TRAVELING WITH YOU!   5

SLIME, GLUE, AND SCIENCE   6-7

IT'S TIME TO SLIME!   8-9

AN INVESTIGATION OF FLUIDS   10

VISCOSITY VS. DENSITY   11

VISCOSITY FOR EVERYONE   12

DENSITY LAYERS   13

NON-NEWTONIAN FLUIDS   14

FLUFFY SLIME!   15

EXPOSED TO RUST   16-17

STAINLESS AS STEEL!   18

LET'S RUST 'EM ALL!   19

GREASY LIKE OIL,
FAT LIKE BUTTER   20-21

LIPIDS – THE REAL TASTE
OF LIFE   22

BUBBLES IN A JAR   23

DARTH SOAP – THE ENEMY OF DIRT	24–25
OIL VS. SOAP	26
A DISTURBANCE IN THE FORCE	27
UNITED AGAINST DIRT	28
MORE THAN SALADS	29
IT'S REACTION TIME!	30
POURING THE GLUE	31
FIGHT AGAINST LIMESCALE	32
DROP BY DROP	33
THE RUBBER EGG	34
THE ART OF LIMESCALE	35
MOLD, MOLD, AND MORE MOLD	36–37
NOBEL PRIZE MOLD	38
THE WORLD OF MOLD	39
MUD AND SLIME!	40
DEPOSITS!	41
BENEATH YOUR FEET	42
PERMEABLE SOIL	43
SO MANY WORMS!	44
WORM HUNT	45
GLOSSARY	46–47

THE SCIENTIFIC METHOD

The **SCIENTIFIC METHOD** is the way in which science investigates the reality around us. It is the most reliable method we know to gain knowledge of things and of the world. It was the scientist **GALILEO GALILEI** who highlighted the importance of this method and gave it visibility in his writings.

Scientific does not mean "accurate"; instead, it means something is **reproducible**, that is, it can be repeated. With the same initial conditions, we expect the experiment to always have the same result. The scientific method is **EXPERIMENTAL**, that is, based on experiments, tests, and observations, and this is the fun part where the scientist becomes creative!

THE MAIN STAGES OF EXPERIMENTAL SCIENTIFIC METHOD ARE:

1. Observing a phenomenon and asking yourself questions.
2. Formulating a hypothesis, that is, a possible explanation of the phenomenon.
3. Carrying out an experiment to check if the hypothesis is correct.
4. Analyzing the results.
5. Repeating the experiment in different ways.
6. Coming to a conclusion and creating a rule.

TRAVELING WITH YOU!

You can call me **PROFESSOR ALBERT**. I am a renowned scientist and a lover of the outdoors and cycling. I'm passionate about life, the universe, and...everything!

My name is **EMMA**. Here's what I love most: going on trips with Professor Albert, candy, and *Star Wars* movies.

I am **GREG THE ROBOT**, an advanced form of artificial intelligence. I have a positronic brain with too many mistakes in it.

TWO WORDS: SAFETY FIRST!

1. Before undertaking any experiment, always read all the instructions carefully.

2. It is forbidden to eat or drink during the experiments and, above all, to eat or drink your experiment! It's a bad idea! Do not do it.

3. Use old clothes, as you will get dirty! Food coloring can stain your clothing and skin.

4. Wash your hands after every experiment. Some substances you use may be harmful to your health.

5. Do not pour slime or sticky compounds down the drain. Use a garbage can.

Some of the scientific activities in the book require adult supervision.

All the words in CAPITAL LETTERS are in the Glossary on pages 46–47, where the terms are explained in more detail.

SLIME, GLUE, AND SCIENCE

HOW LONG HAS SLIME BEEN AROUND?

It's more than 40 years old! The first time slime appeared was in the mid-seventies. It was green and sold in a small plastic jar shaped like a garbage can. Slime was an instant success, and since then it's been sold in different colors, scents, and textures.

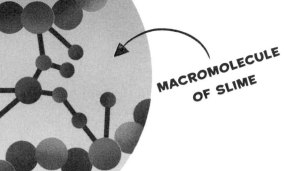

MACROMOLECULE
OF SLIME

CHEMISTRY OF SLIME

Sticky, moist, soft, and rubbery. Slime is the result of a special chemical reaction that makes it slippery.

Liquid glue, the main ingredient of slime, is made up of POLYMERS. These MOLECULES are similar to long, identical chains, and they move freely over each other, making the glue liquid!

By adding the activating SOLUTION to the glue and vigorously stirring it, a CHEMICAL REACTION is triggered. Bonds form between the chains, which are intertwined to create a network.

LIQUID OR SOLID STATE?

Slime is not a normal FLUID. Some of its strange characteristics earned it the status of **NON-NEWTONIAN FLUID**! Depending on how it is manipulated, it changes its state.

FREE

Without a force that compresses it, if we allow slime to flow between our fingers, it will slide like a liquid...

COMPRESSED

...but, if we manipulate it by stretching or crushing it, it will behave like a solid!

AT THE MOVIES!

In the movie *Ghostbusters*, released in 1984, Slimer made his debut. He's a greedy and chubby ghost that leaves his green and gelatinous trail everywhere.

IT'S TIME TO SLIME!

YOU WILL NEED

- clear glue and vinyl glue
- shaving foam
- baking soda
- food coloring
- liquid laundry detergent
- a bowl
- a spoon

DIFFICULTY:

DIRTINESS:

TIME: *10–15 minutes +10–15 min. resting*

DO IT WITH:

HOW TO DO IT

1 Pour 3 tablespoons of clear glue and 3 tablespoons of vinyl glue into a bowl. Add a handful of shaving foam and food coloring and start mixing with a spoon.

2 Add 1 tablespoon of baking soda and 1 tablespoon of detergent and continue stirring vigorously.

NOW, LET'S MIX!

FUN FACT

You can add glitter to make your slime even brighter.

EXPERIMENT SUCCESSFUL!

(3) Leave the mixture to rest for 15 minutes, then start mixing again. Add another spoonful of detergent if it doesn't thicken in a short time.

(4) Finally, knead the slime with your hands as if it were dough.

WHAT HAPPENS

When adding baking soda and detergent, the reaction that turns liquid glue into a gelatinous and slimy paste is triggered. Remember: Resting time is critical. Try several times if you don't succeed the first time. Go for it!

AN INVESTIGATION OF FLUIDS

WHAT IS VISCOSITY?

When falling, water and honey behave differently. Water falls quickly because it is not viscous. Honey falls slowly, first at the center then on the sides, because it is very viscous. VISCOSITY is the ability of a FLUID to resist sliding, that is, the tendency to drag with it all its particles when it slides along a **surface**.

TEMPERATURE AND VISCOSITY

Heat alters the VISCOSITY of a substance. Viscosity decreases with the increase of temperature. For example, if you heat some honey in a pan or in a microwave, you will see its texture change. **Does its viscosity increase or decrease?**

SOLID HONEY

FLUID HONEY

COLD   HOT

WHAT IS DENSITY?

The DENSITY of a substance is described as the ratio between MASS and VOLUME! Mass indicates the amount of matter present in a substance, and volume indicates how much space matter occupies.

VISCOSITY VS. DENSITY

FLUIDS are divided into Newtonians and non-Newtonians. These categories are named for **ISAAC NEWTON**, who discovered a formula that describes their behavior.

Isaac Newton

E<small>QUAL VOLUME</small> / D<small>IFFERENT MASS</small>

DENSITY also depends on temperature. While MASS does not vary with temperature, VOLUME does. This means that, as temperature increases, the material may expand (increase in volume), becoming less dense, or it may contract (decrease in volume), becoming denser.

WATER IS AN EXCEPTION!

When temperature decreases and water becomes ice, it decreases in DENSITY and increases in VOLUME, and vice versa. This is why ice is less dense than water and floats in it.

E<small>QUAL MASS</small> / D<small>IFFERENT VOLUME</small>

DENSER IS NOT ALWAYS MORE VISCOUS

DENSITY and VISCOSITY are not always related: For example, oil can be less dense than water, but much more VISCOUS.

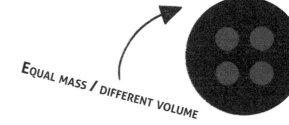

VISCOSITY FOR EVERYONE

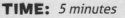
YOU WILL NEED

- 1 glass of water
- 1 glass of liquid honey
- 2 teaspoons
- stopwatch

HOW TO DO IT

1 Put a spoon into the water glass.

2 Fill the spoon with as much water as possible and lift it over the glass.

3 Tilt the spoon slightly and let all the water drop back into the glass.

4 Using the stopwatch, note how many seconds it takes to empty the spoon completely.

5 Do the same experiment with honey.

YOUR TURN TO TRY!

Find other types of liquids at home and see if they behave more like water or honey.

WHAT HAPPENS

You are watching a direct effect of VISCOSITY. Being more VISCOUS, honey takes longer to fall from the spoon.

12

DENSITY LAYERS

YOU WILL NEED

- 1 glass jar
(such as a tomato sauce jar)
- honey
- water
- food coloring
(we recommend blue)
- dish soap
- oil (sunflower, peanut,
or olive oil—your choice)
- denatured alcohol
(the one used to clean and
disinfect)
- 1 cap or lid, to close the jar

HOW TO DO IT

1 Dissolve a few drops of food coloring in the water.

2 Pour the following liquids very slowly, so as to create a 1 in (2.5 cm) layer of each: honey, dish soap, colored water, oil, alcohol.

3 Close the bottle with the cap so you can keep it over time.

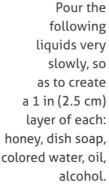

WARNING!

Pour the first 2 liquids (honey and dish soap) **into the center of the jar, without touching its walls.** *For the remaining liquids (colored water, oil, and alcohol),* **tilt the jar and pour them against the walls of the container.** *Be careful not to shake the bottle or turn it upside down, to prevent the various liquids from mixing.*

WHAT HAPPENS

Liquids are arranged one on top of the other according to their DENSITY. The liquids or substances with higher density sink when immersed in FLUIDS with lower DENSITY, and vice versa.

NON-NEWTONIAN FLUIDS

Apart from slime, there are other examples of NON-NEWTONIAN FLUIDS that are easy to find in everyday life. These include ketchup, blood, paint, and toothpaste. Others are more dangerous and difficult to find, like quicksand!

DIFFICULTY:

DIRTINESS:

TIME: 5–10 minutes

DO IT WITH:

YOU WILL NEED

- corn starch (or potato starch)
- water
- bowl
- glass
- food coloring (if you want)

WHAT HAPPENS

Quickly tap on the substance, using your finger or a spoon. What happens? And what if you touch the substance slowly instead?

If you tap the substance quickly, it will feel harder, while if you touch it gently, it will behave more like a liquid.

HOW TO DO IT

1 Pour 2 glasses of starch into the bowl.

2 Slowly pour 2 glasses of water in, mixing the substance until you obtain a thick mixture.

3 Find your favorite consistency and add a bit more water or starch if needed.

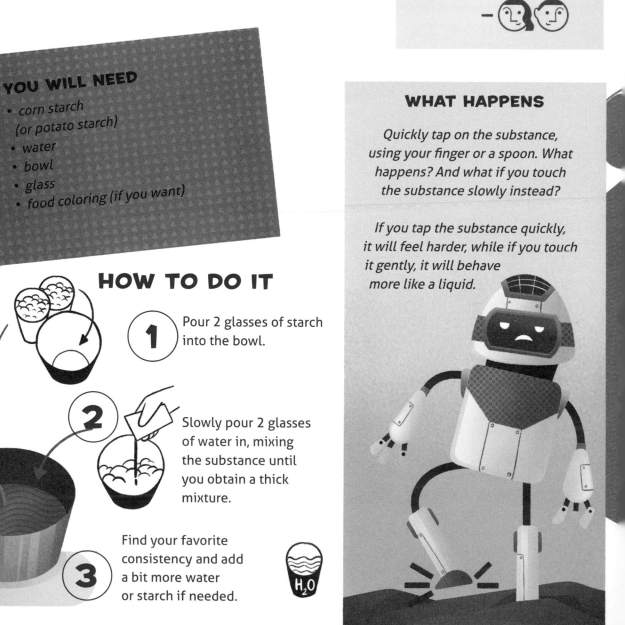

FLUFFY SLIME!

HOW TO DO IT

YOU WILL NEED

- *kitchen scale*
- *0.1 oz (3 g) of borax*
- *water*
- *0.7 oz (20 g) of clear glue*
- *0.7 oz (20 g) of shaving foam*
- *0.3 oz (10 g) of dish soap*
- *food coloring*

1

Heat 2.8 oz (80 g) of water in a saucepan and then add 0.1 oz (3 g) of borax. Mix well: your activator is ready!

2

Pour the clear glue, shaving foam, and dish detergent into a bowl. Mix very well and add food coloring as desired.

3

When the mixture becomes smooth, add 3 teaspoons of activator and stir for a few minutes.

4

In a short amount of time, the mixture will become more and more stringy. When it is no longer sticky, take it in your hands and start kneading it as if you were making a ball. Continue for a few minutes, until the slime reaches the desired consistency.

WHAT HAPPENS

The borax that you added as an activator fits between the filament chains of the glue to form the gelatinous net, typical of slime.

EXPOSED TO RUST

WHY IS RUST FORMED?

Red and lumpy, rust forms and corrodes iron objects when we leave them exposed to air and humidity for a long time. But how is it formed?

Rust is the product of a CHEMICAL REACTION called **OXIDATION**.

Iron reacts with the oxygen in air and water,
in the form of humidity or rain. With the help of carbon
dioxide in the atmosphere, iron turns into a lumpy
and flaky substance. It detaches, revealing
the underlying part that remains continuously exposed
to the process until it is completely consumed.
THIS IS RUST!

> **IRON**

OXIDATION SCALE
Not all materials have
the same tendency to
oxidize. Chemists have
defined a scale to compare
this feature.

> **ALUMINUM**

> **ZINC**

> **CHROMIUM**

HOW TO PROTECT AGAINST RUST

*The most common systems to protect against
rust are galvanization and chrome plating.
These systems allow the material to be coated
with a layer of zinc or chromium, leaving
the underlying iron intact. That's how
we protect cars, motorcycles, and bikes!*

This gentleman is
SIR HUMPHRY DAVY.
He was the one who discovered
how to protect iron!

STAINLESS AS STEEL!

Cr

Among the many metals that surround us, some are a potent force against rust!

Stainless steel contains a small amount of chromium, which makes it stainless, i.e., better resistant to OXIDATION and corrosion, the phenomena that cause rust. Chromium, reacting with oxygen, is able to coat itself in a whitish layer that protects the underlying metal from the corrosive action of external agents.

Steel is a METAL ALLOY, mainly composed of iron and a small percentage (2%) of carbon.

TYPES OF ALLOYS

An alloy is a mixture of two or more elements, one of which is a metal.

IRON + CARBON = STEEL
IRON + CARBON + CHROMIUM = STAINLESS STEEL
COPPER + ZINC = BRASS
COPPER + TIN = BRONZE

The new material obtained has metallic properties that differ from those of the individual components.
For example, steel is more resistant than iron; brass is harder than copper and shinier than zinc.

LET'S RUST 'EM ALL!

YOU WILL NEED

- 4 glasses
- water
- 1 teaspoon of salt
- oil
- vinegar
- 4 nails or 4 pieces of iron (Caution! Do not use galvanized material)

HOW TO DO IT

1 Fill the four glasses: the first with water, the second with water and salt, the third with vinegar, the fourth with oil.

2 Put a nail or a piece of iron in each glass.

3 Look at the glasses every day and check what happens. Which nail rusts first?

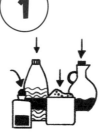 What happens after 2 days? And after 4 days?

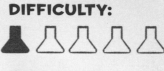

DIFFICULTY:

DIRTINESS:

TIME: 5 minutes + 3–4 days

DO IT WITH: —

WHAT HAPPENS

Rust is formed when iron is exposed to air and water, so where there is no water, there is no rust. Salt accelerates the rusting process because it helps water to act faster.

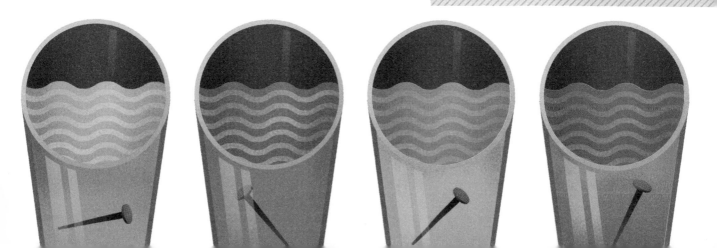

GREASY LIKE OIL, FAT LIKE BUTTER

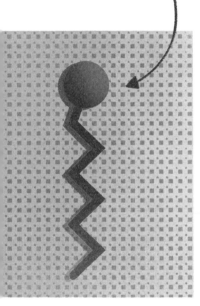

SATURATED FATTY ACID

WHAT ARE GREASE AND FAT?

Yep! Even our kitchen hides a lot of disgusting things, not just tasty treats!

The grease we find in the kitchen is mainly made of oils and fats, which contain MOLECULES called FATTY ACIDS. These acids are formed by a long chain of CARBON ATOMS, joined together by two types of bonds.

Simple bonds generate straight chains, typical of SATURATED FATTY ACIDS. Double bonds, on the other hand, produce crooked chains, typical of UNSATURATED FATTY ACIDS.

It is these **bonds** that determine the different characteristics of fat!
For example, the greater the number of double bonds, the lower the temperature at which the fat melts.

IT'S ALL FAT!

UNSATURATED FATTY ACID

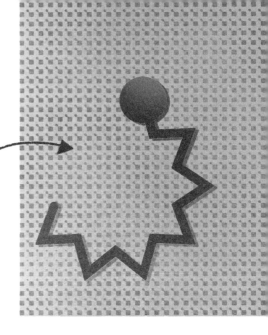

WHY IS BUTTER SOLID AND OIL LIQUID?

In the animal world, SATURATED FATTY ACIDS—such as butter and lard—predominate, while in the vegetable world, UNSATURATED FATTY ACIDS—such as olive oil and almond oil—predominate.

Fats—without double bonds—are solid at room temperature, while oils—rich in double bonds—are liquid at room temperature.

LIPIDS – THE REAL TASTE OF LIFE

Fats and oils are part of a large family that chemists call LIPIDS.

Meat, fish, and eggs contain fat because they are all derived from animals, which, like us, use LIPIDS for their vital functions. Animals use fats as an energy reserve, for thermal insulation, and in making cellular structures.

SIMILAR DISSOLVES SIMILAR!

Lipids are not soluble, that is, they do not dissolve well in water. However, they are soluble in other substances similar to them, such as acetone, alcohols, and hydrocarbons (gasoline). This is why we must use specific products to remove lipids from pots, pans, and clothes!

Waxes are also lipids. They constitute the thin layer that covers leaves and fruits of some plants to limit the dispersion of water and as a protection against pests. Waxes are part of the skeleton of many insects and cover the plumage of waterfowl.

BUBBLES IN A JAR

YOU WILL NEED

- 1 glass
- water
- oil (corn, sunflower, or peanut, your choice)
- food coloring
- 1 teaspoon
- 1 effervescent tablet (for example, aspirin)

HOW TO DO IT

DIFFICULTY:

DIRTINESS:

TIME: 5–10 minutes

DO IT WITH:

1 Fill a third of the glass with water.

2 Add a few drops of food coloring and mix well with the spoon.

3 Fill the remaining two-thirds of the glass by pouring the oil very slowly, taking care not to create bubbles.

4 Wait a few moments so that the liquids separate well.

5 Put the aspirin tablet into the glass and watch what happens.

WHAT HAPPENS

Water and oil are immiscible liquids, that is, they do not mix with each other. The tablet in contact with water releases gas bubbles, which bind to the water and transport it to the surface. In contact with air, the gas bubbles burst, and the water, which is denser than the oil, sinks again, so the cycle starts all over.

DARTH SOAP – THE ENEMY OF DIRT

The worst enemy of the galaxy of dirt is soap. It is the product of a CHEMICAL REACTION, called SAPONIFICATION.

SOAP HAS TWO BIG FORCES!

The MOLECULES that compose soap have a double nature:

• a **hydrophilic head**, which binds well to water;
• a **hydrophobic tail**, which repels water and attracts fatty and oily substances.

When the MOLECULES of soap meet dirt, they arrange themselves in a circular way, with the tails turned inward—in contact with the dirt—and the heads turned outward, in contact with the water. This way, a small sphere called a MICELLE is created.

CLEAN! OR CLEAN NOT. THERE IS NO RINSING.

The secret of the cleaning power of soap is in the MICELLES! This particular arrangement allows soap to trap dirt.

Soap is able to break the SURFACE TENSION, that is, the invisible and elastic "membrane" that forms on the surface of a liquid. For this reason, soap is also called a SURFACTANT.

THE ART OF WALKING ON WATER

Some insects manage to float and walk on water using SURFACE TENSION, that is, this cohesion force between MOLECULES.

OIL VS. SOAP

YOU WILL NEED

- 1 glass
- water
- oil
- 1 tbsp of dishwashing soap
- 1 tsp, to mix

HOW TO DO IT

1 Fill the glass halfway with water. H_2O

2 Add oil up to a third of the glass.

3 Mix and watch what happens for a few moments.

4 When the two liquids have separated, add a spoonful of dish soap, then mix and observe the result.

WHAT HAPPENS

We know that water and oil don't mix, but when we add soap, it traps the oil droplets in its micelles, allowing oil to mix with water.

A DISTURBANCE IN THE FORCE

YOU WILL NEED
- 1 clear bowl
- water
- ground pepper
- dishwashing soap

DIFFICULTY:

DIRTINESS:

TIME: 5–10 minutes

DO IT WITH:

HOW TO DO IT

I AM WALKING ON WATER!

1 Fill the clear bowl with water from the tap.

2 Carefully pour the pepper in, spreading it over the entire surface, and observe how it is arranged.

3 Put a drop of detergent into the center of the bowl and watch carefully.

WHAT HAPPENS

At first, the pepper remains on the surface of the water because it is very light and cannot break the SURFACE TENSION of the liquid. Soap breaks this "membrane," causing the pepper to fall to the bottom.

27

UNITED AGAINST DIRT

WARNING, WARNING!

Unassuming cooking ingredients can reveal a lot of surprises!
Baking soda looks like a fine white powder.
It is a BASE that is used in many ways!

1 IT HELPS TO FIGHT DIRT

Baking soda makes soap more efficient.
That's because baking soda is a BASE,
and its sandy consistency makes it
slightly abrasive. However, it cannot
remove grease on its own.

2 IT ABSORBS ODORS

Unlike deodorants or candles,
which mask odors, baking soda
absorbs odors.

3 IT HAS CLEANING POWER

That's why it is used
in laundry and in
whitening toothpastes
to remove stains.

4 IT PRODUCES GAS

When heated above 212°F
(100°C), baking soda releases
carbon dioxide, making it an
excellent extinguisher because
it stifles the oxygen of a fire.

$NaHCO_3$

MORE THAN SALADS

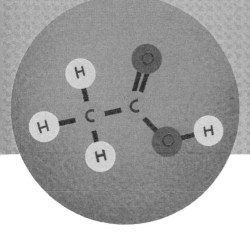

Vinegar, in addition to being a dressing on salads, also has other talents!
It is an ACID, and this characteristic makes it a good detergent.

FUN FACT

If it is too concentrated, vinegar can corrode some materials, such as marble, stone, and rubber.
Vinegar can also be very aggressive on some metals, such as cast iron, aluminum, and steel, releasing irritants of the skin.
The word "vinegar" comes from the Old French *vinaigre*, meaning "sour wine."

SPARKLING AND EFFERVESCENT MIXTURES!

Have you ever tried mixing vinegar with baking soda?
The mixture releases water and carbon dioxide, accompanied by a magnificent, effervescent foam!
However, it is not a useful reaction to fight dirt; if we mix acids and bases together, they cancel each other out and are not very effective.

IT'S REACTION TIME!

DIFFICULTY:

DIRTINESS:

TIME: *10–15 minutes + 4–5 hours*

DO IT WITH:

HOW TO DO IT

1 Put 2 teaspoons of baking soda in each glass.

2 Fill the first glass halfway with vinegar.

3 In the second glass, put 2 teaspoons of cream of tartar and add half a glass of water at room temperature.

4 In the third glass, add 2 teaspoons of honey and mix well.

5 In the fourth glass, fill it halfway with boiling water.

WHAT HAPPENS

Not all reactions between an ACID and a BASE take place at the same rate: some develop earlier, others later.

Glass 1	Glass 2	Glass 3	Glass 4
The reaction took place quickly, and the carbon dioxide that was released vanished just as fast.	*The reaction is slower, and carbon dioxide is released minutes later.*	*Honey is very viscous; it will not be able to immediately develop carbon dioxide. It will take a few hours.*	*The reaction is instantaneous, and the carbon dioxide produced evaporates immediately.*

POURING THE GLUE

HOW TO DO IT

YOU WILL NEED
- 1 glass of milk
- 4 spoons of white vinegar
- 1 tablespoon of baking soda
- water
- 1 saucepan
- 1 strainer

1 Heat the milk in a saucepan.

2 Remove from heat, add 4 tbsp of white vinegar, stir, and wait for 10 minutes.

3 Filter the liquid using a strainer and wait for 10 minutes.

4 Pour the lumpy mixture in the saucepan.

5 Add a tablespoon of baking soda and 4–5 tablespoons of water, to dissolve everything.

6 Stir and heat the mixture over medium-low heat until it starts to boil.

7 When the mixture boils, turn off the heat and let it cool.

8 You will get a slightly viscous liquid substance that you can use as a glue.

Don't get discouraged if it doesn't work right away! The glue needs a few hours to stick.

WHAT HAPPENS

The vinegar thickens the milk by separating it into a liquid and a solid part. The baking soda in contact with the ACID curd turns it into a sticky and pasty glue, releasing gas bubbles.

FIGHT AGAINST LIMESCALE

What is that **whitish** layer that forms on the surface of sinks, tiles, and appliances in contact with water?
THAT'S LIMESCALE.
Limescale is a rock, whose main component is **calcium carbonate**.

During its cycle, water comes into contact with rocks, bringing with it the minerals contained in them such as **CALCIUM CARBONATE, MAGNESIUM,** and **BICARBONATES.** These minerals are then deposited during evaporation, forming limescale incrustations.

Day after day, drop by drop, the calcium carbonate present in running water accumulates, creating small grains that can clog and damage pipes. Limescale is dissolved by acids, which is why vinegar is excellent for removing it!

DROP BY DROP

Water is capable of great work! Drop by drop, it can create magnificent sculptures: stalactites and stalagmites.

Stalactites and **stalagmites** are produced by the dripping of water, which deposits minerals over time. When it rains, water is enriched with carbon dioxide present in the atmosphere, thus becoming slightly ACID. This SOLUTION dissolves the calcium carbonate contained in the rocks, transforming it into calcium bicarbonate. Inside caves, water evaporates, carbon dioxide is released, and calcium bicarbonate becomes calcium carbonate, which solidifies and forms stalactites.

FUN FACTS

The name **STALACTITE** derives from the Greek word *stalaktites*, which means "dripping." Geologists call the structures that hang from the ceiling of caves stalactites, while they call those that rise from the floor of the cave stalagmites. Over time (a lot of time!), both structures grow until they join to form columns of calcium carbonate.

THE RUBBER EGG

YOU WILL NEED
- 1 glass
- 1 egg
- vinegar
- 1 saucepan
- water

HOW TO DO IT

1 Put the egg in the saucepan and pour a glass of water over it.

2 Boil for 10 minutes, until the egg becomes hard.

3 Let it cool down, then put the egg in the glass.

4 Pour vinegar into the glass, until it completely covers the egg.

5 Leave the egg in the vinegar for a whole day.

6 Remove the egg from the glass, rinse it, and start playing with it!

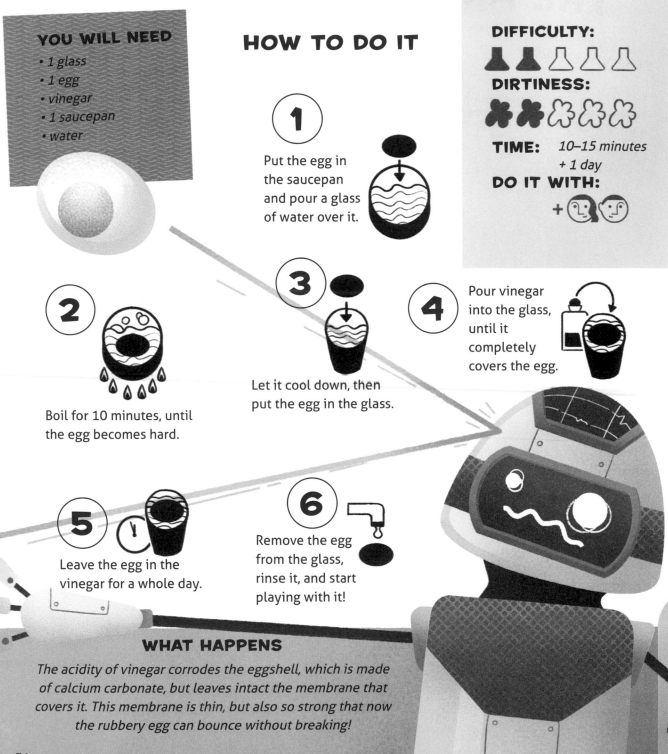

WHAT HAPPENS

The acidity of vinegar corrodes the eggshell, which is made of calcium carbonate, but leaves intact the membrane that covers it. This membrane is thin, but also so strong that now the rubbery egg can bounce without breaking!

THE ART OF LIMESCALE

YOU WILL NEED

- 17 fl oz (500 ml) of water
- 1.4 oz (40 g) of baking soda
- thick wool yarn, about 20 in (50 cm) long
- 2 glass jars
- 1 saucepan
- 1 tray

HOW TO DO IT

DIFFICULTY:

DIRTINESS:

TIME: *10–15 minutes + 7–10 days*

DO IT WITH:

1 Place the two jars on a tray about 6–8 in (15–20 cm) away from each other.

2 In a saucepan, boil 17 fl oz (500 ml) of water.

3 Remove from heat and gradually pour the baking soda in. Stir to dissolve well.

4 Pour the solution into the jars and wait for it to cool down.

5 Tie a knot in the center of the yarn and a few knots at the ends, to create a small weight.

6 Place an end of the yarn in each of the jars and let it sit a few days without touching it.

Bubbles and foam can form, as a result of carbon dioxide being freed from baking soda touching boiling water.

NOTE

Crystals are hard to form because of the heat, cold, and moisture affecting the result. Don't get discouraged!

WHAT HAPPENS

The water rich in baking soda eventually evaporates, and the baking soda crystallizes on the yarn, creating a small stalactite, just as it happens in caves!

MOLD, MOLD, AND MORE MOLD!

If you leave fruit or cheese for some time in a closed container in the fridge or pantry, you will see that after a few days a whitish or greenish spongy spot forms on its surface. **LET ME INTRODUCE YOU TO MOLD!**

Mold is a microorganism belonging to the mushroom family. This family includes many types of **MOLDS, YEASTS, AND FUNGI.**

Mold appears as a **SPONGY MASS** of different colors (black, green, brown, red, blue, yellow), depending on the species and the environmental conditions in which it develops. It is made up of many filaments (hyphae) intertwined with each other. These filaments perform the function of exploration, anchoring, and absorption of nutrients.

In unfavorable environmental conditions, some hyphae are able to turn into spores. This is a means of survival, since spores are ready to come back to life as soon as the environmental conditions suitable for reproducing are found again.

A SPORE OF MOLD

Spores are light, invisible, and incredibly resistant particles that spread in the air, carried by wind, water, and insects.
Mold settles on the surfaces in houses and develops in closed and humid environments, such as cellars and bathrooms.
It is able to grow on non-fresh food kept in unventilated places or inside containers and refrigerators.

Some molds are unpleasant and can cause health problems, while others are edible, like those found in some aged cheeses. Other molds are even useful to defend against bacteria.

NOBEL PRIZE MOLD

It may seem incredible, but mold gave **ALEXANDER FLEMING**,
a British physician and a biologist, the Nobel Prize in Medicine in 1945.

In 1928, Fleming was conducting research on bacteria grown in special containers. He went away on vacation for a few days, and, when he returned, he noticed that one of the bacteria had been contaminated by a fungus and that bacteria did not grow in that area. Fleming sensed that mold could be the cause of death of the bacteria, and therefore he started studying mold, obtaining a substance that he called penicillin.
PENICILLIN IS THE ANCESTOR OF ANTIBIOTICS, AND IT HAS ALLOWED US TO DEFEAT VARIOUS DISEASES.

Thirty-five years earlier, an Italian doctor, **VINCENZO TIBERIO**, had already discovered the beneficial effects of this mold.
He noticed that every time a well near a house was cleaned of mold, people who drank that water had bowel problems that stopped only when the mold reappeared. Tiberio published his results in a scientific journal, but unfortunately his discovery was ignored.

THE WORLD OF MOLD

YOU WILL NEED

- 1 plastic container with a lid (approx. 3 fl oz / 100 ml)
- 1/4 of a bouillon cube
- 1 teaspoon of sugar
- 0.03 oz (1 g) of agar-agar
- water
- 1 saucepan
- 1 cotton swab

HOW TO DO IT

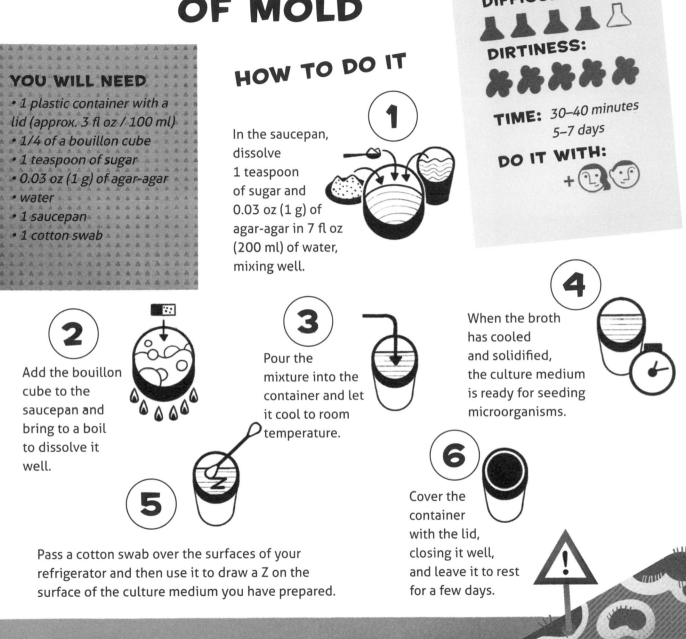

1 In the saucepan, dissolve 1 teaspoon of sugar and 0.03 oz (1 g) of agar-agar in 7 fl oz (200 ml) of water, mixing well.

2 Add the bouillon cube to the saucepan and bring to a boil to dissolve it well.

3 Pour the mixture into the container and let it cool to room temperature.

4 When the broth has cooled and solidified, the culture medium is ready for seeding microorganisms.

5 Pass a cotton swab over the surfaces of your refrigerator and then use it to draw a Z on the surface of the culture medium you have prepared.

6 Cover the container with the lid, closing it well, and leave it to rest for a few days.

WHAT HAPPENS

The culture medium you have prepared is a soil ready to grow many types of mold, yeast, and bacteria present in the air and in the surrounding environment.

WARNING!

Never open the container! Just observe it, and then throw everything in the trash!

MUD AND SLIME!

Mud can be slimy. It can make your feet sink into the ground on a rainy day, or it can be creamy and spreadable, and used as a beauty remedy!

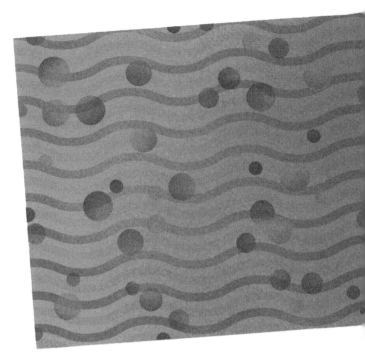

MUD

Mud is a mixture of earth, dust, and very fine solid material dispersed in a very small amount of liquid. If such a mixture rests for some time, the dispersed substances settle on the bottom, forming the mud.

ACTIVATED SLUDGE

Activated sludge is a process used to purify dirty water from domestic wastewater. The bacteria contained in the sludge feed on organic matter and turn it into other simpler substances, such as carbon dioxide and water. This way, the bacteria obtain energy that they use to grow and multiply.

THERMAL MUD

Thermal mud is rich in clay, minerals, and algae with many beneficial properties. The mud is used in the form of a compress so that the nutrients of the mud enter the skin, while the waste substances produced by the body are absorbed by the mud.

DEPOSITS!

HOW TO DO IT

YOU WILL NEED
- *gravel*
- *clay*
- *sand*
- *gardening soil*
- *water*
- *1 bowl*
- *1 clear jar at least 15 in (40 cm) high*

1 Fill 3/4 of the jar with water.

2 In a bowl, mix different quantities of gravel, clay, sand, and soil (3–4 tablespoons) to fill 1–2 glasses.

3 Slowly pour the mixture into the jar containing water and observe.

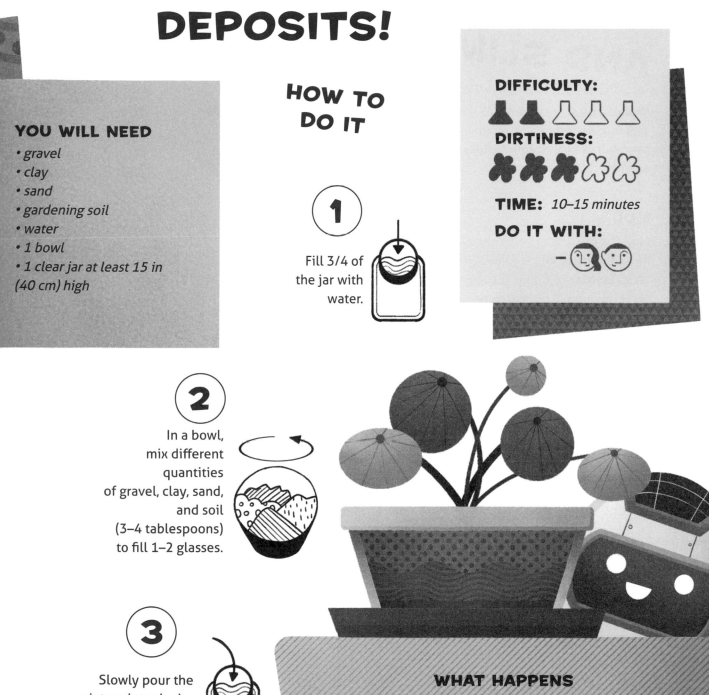

WHAT HAPPENS
You will see the largest and heaviest particles, such as gravel, fall to the bottom, while the clay remains in suspension in the water and slowly settles to form the most superficial layer.

BENEATH YOUR FEET

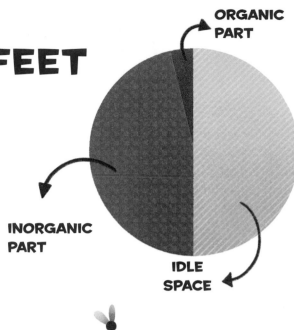

ORGANIC PART

INORGANIC PART

IDLE SPACE

WHAT IS THE SOIL BENEATH YOUR FEET MADE OF?

Soil is a mixture of inorganic and organic substances that covers the surface of the earth. The **INORGANIC PART** (about 45–50%) is formed by minerals contained in rocks. The **ORGANIC PART** (about 5–10%), called humus, is made of leaves, seeds, and animal remains, which make the soil very fertile. The remaining 50% of the soil is made up of **IDLE SPACE**, which is filled with air and water depending on the type of soil and the environmental conditions—temperature, humidity, precipitation—in which it is found.

SOIL PERMEABILITY:

PERMEABILITY is the ability of the soil to let water pass through it. The more the ground contains voids, or spaces, the more permeable it is.

GRAVELLY
Water flows through it easily.

SANDY
Permeable; it allows water to pass through.

CLAY
Impermeable; it does not allow water to pass through.

MIXED
Gravel, sand, and clay; more or less fertile and suitable to be cultivated.

PERMEABLE SOIL

YOU WILL NEED

- three 2-liter plastic bottles
- 1 glass of sand
- 1 glass of clay
- 1 glass of garden soil
- water
- gauze
- 3 elastic bands
- scissors

DIFFICULTY:

DIRTINESS:

TIME: 15–20 minutes

DO IT WITH:

HOW TO DO IT

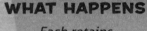

1

Cut off the upper part of each bottle to obtain a funnel about 1/3 of the height of the whole bottle. Remove the caps.

2

Cover the neck of each bottle with the same amount of gauze (three layers per bottle is enough), and secure them with an elastic band to create a cap.

3

Place one funnel inside the bottom of each bottle.

4

Fill bottle A with sand, bottle B with clay, and bottle C with gardening soil.

5

Pour 1 cup of water in each funnel and wait for 10 minutes, observing what happens.

WHAT HAPPENS

Each retains water in a different way: Water passes quickly through the sand, slower through the gardening soil, and even slower through the clay.

SO MANY WORMS!

It's easy to say "worms"! Actually, we use this term for a lot of animals with a narrow, elongated, and legless appearance, which belong to different groups. We also mistakenly call the larvae of other insects, such as flies, worms. Certainly, because of their appearance, not everyone loves worms.

TO EACH THEIR OWN NICKNAME

Worms have different names according to their characteristics: roundworms (*Nematodes*), flatworms (*Platyhelminthes*), ringed worms (*Annelids*). There is also a worm nicknamed "Christmas tree" (*Spirobranchus giganteus*) because of its shape and colors.

FUN FACT

Earthworms are probably the best known worms, but you may not know that they are also very useful! They make the soil more fertile by constantly digging tunnels, mixing it, and allowing water, air, and roots to penetrate better.

WORM HUNT

DIFFICULTY:

DIRTINESS:

TIME: 10–15 minutes

DO IT WITH:

YOU WILL NEED

- 0.07 oz (2 g) of sodium alginate
- water
- 0.07 oz (2 g) of calcium chloride or dehumidifying salt
- 2 glasses or bowls
- hand blender
- food coloring
- spoon and/or syringe without needle

It is not a good idea to play with the worms in the garden. Here is a nice experiment to create DIY worms, without scaring your friends or disturbing the earthworms.

HOW TO DO IT

1

Pour 0.07 oz (2 g) of sodium alginate into 7 fl oz (200 ml) of water.

2 Add some food coloring.

3 Blend everything until the alginate is well dissolved.

4 Pour 0.07 oz (2 g) of calcium chloride into 7 fl oz (200 ml) of water and mix well to dissolve it.

5 Using a spoon or a syringe without a needle, pour small quantities of alginate solution into the calcium chloride solution, and you will see gelatinous worms forming.

6 Leave to soak for a few minutes and then drain your worms and play with them.

NOTE

The longer you leave alginate in contact with calcium chloride, the more the solution thickens, making hardier and more bouncy worms.

WHAT HAPPENS

Sodium alginate is made from seaweed. When sodium alginate comes into contact with calcium chloride, it forms bonds between the MOLECULES. These bonds make a sort of film around water, therefore creating small, sticky worms.

GLOSSARY

ACID: Substance with a sour taste capable of corroding metals. Acids have a pH value between 0 and 6 and are chemically the opposite of a base. Some acids are weak, such as those present in vinegar or lemons, while others are strong and dangerous, like hydrochloric acid found in our stomachs.

ATOM: A tiny particle that matter is made of.

BASE: A corrosive substance with a bitter taste, used in detergents. Chemically, it is the opposite of an acid. Some bases are weak, like baking soda, while others are strong and dangerous, like caustic soda.

CHEMICAL REACTION: A process in which two or more substances, called reagents, combine together to form new substances that are called products.

DENSITY: A characteristic of materials and substances, given by the ratio between mass and volume.

FLUID: A substance that occurs in a liquid or gas state. For example: water or air.

LIPIDS: Generic term to indicate fats and oils, substances not soluble in water and found in living organisms.

MASS: The quantity of matter contained in a substance.

METAL ALLOY: A mixture of two or more elements, one of which is a metal.

MICELLE: A set of molecules, with a hydrophilic head and a hydrophobic tail, that come together as a sphere.

MOLECULE: A set of two or more atoms held together by bonds.

NON-NEWTONIAN FLUIDS: Substances that do not comply to the properties of fluids as described by Newton.

OXIDATION: A chemical reaction in which a substance transfers electrons to another substance.

PERMEABILITY: The ability of some substances and materials to let water pass through them.

POLYMER: A large molecule formed by a chain of many repeated base units (components).

SAPONIFICATION: The chemical reaction from which soap is obtained.

SOLUTION: A homogeneous mixture in which the different components are uniformly distributed. Some examples are salt water from the sea, or air, which is a mixture of gas.

SURFACE TENSION: The invisible and elastic force that forms on the surface of a liquid due to the strong attraction of its molecules.

SURFACTANT: A substance, such soap, that has the ability to break the surface tension of a liquid.

VISCOSITY: A property that indicates the resistance of the particles of a substance when sliding over each other.

VOLUME: The space occupied by a substance.

VALERIA BARATTINI

Valeria holds a master's degree in Economics and Management of Arts and Cultural Activities from the University of Ca' Foscari in Venice, and a master's in Standards for Museum Education from the Roma Tre University. She works in education and cultural planning. Since 2015, she has been working in partnership with Fosforo, hosting events and activities in the field of scientific dissemination and informal teaching.

MATTIA CRIVELLINI

A graduate of Computer Science at the University of Bologna, Mattia has been studying Cognitive Sciences in the United States at Indiana University. Since 2011, he has been the director of Fosforo, the science festival of Senigallia. He organizes and plans activities, conferences, and shows for communication and dissemination of science in Italy and abroad through the NEXT Cultural Association.

FRANCESCA GORINI

After obtaining a master's degree in Industrial Biotechnology from the University of Urbino "Carlo Bo" and doing an internship in Cambridge (UK), Francesca obtained a PhD in Molecular Medicine at the Vita Salute San Raffaele University in Milan. She has dedicated herself to research in various laboratories and to the management of clinical studies in hospitals. She teaches in schools and collaborates with Fosforo in scientific dissemination.

ROSSELLA TRIONFETTI

Since she was a child, Rossella has been going to bookstores and libraries in search of illustrated books on animals, having immediately shown interest in drawing and everything that surrounds it. After graduating in Applied Arts, she specialized in the field of illustration and graphics, attending various courses with professionals in the sector, including at the Mimaster of Milan. Currently, she works as an illustrator of children's books and also collaborates in the creation of apps. In recent years, she has illustrated several books for White Star Kids.

Valeria, Mattia, Francesca, and Rossella are all part of
FOSFORO: THE SCIENCE FESTIVAL.

Fosforo: It's a fair, a festival, a meeting place. It's a series of events to give stimuli, overturn the commonplace, make people fall in love with science, and stimulate them to dream, think, invent, and discover. *Fosforo:* It's scientific dissemination. An event with national and international guests, who, since 2011, have been animating Senigallia, in the Marche region of Italy, for 4 days in May. This is done with surprising scientific exhibitions, laboratories, and conferences on the main scientific topics.

White Star Kids® is a registered trademark property of White Star s.r.l.

© 2020 White Star s.r.l.
Piazzale Luigi Cadorna, 6 - 20123 Milan, Italy
www.whitestar.it

Translation and editing: TperTradurre, Rome, Italy
Editing: Michele Suchomel-Casey

ISBN 978-88-544-1727-4
2 3 4 5 6   27 26 25 24 23

Printed in Slovenia

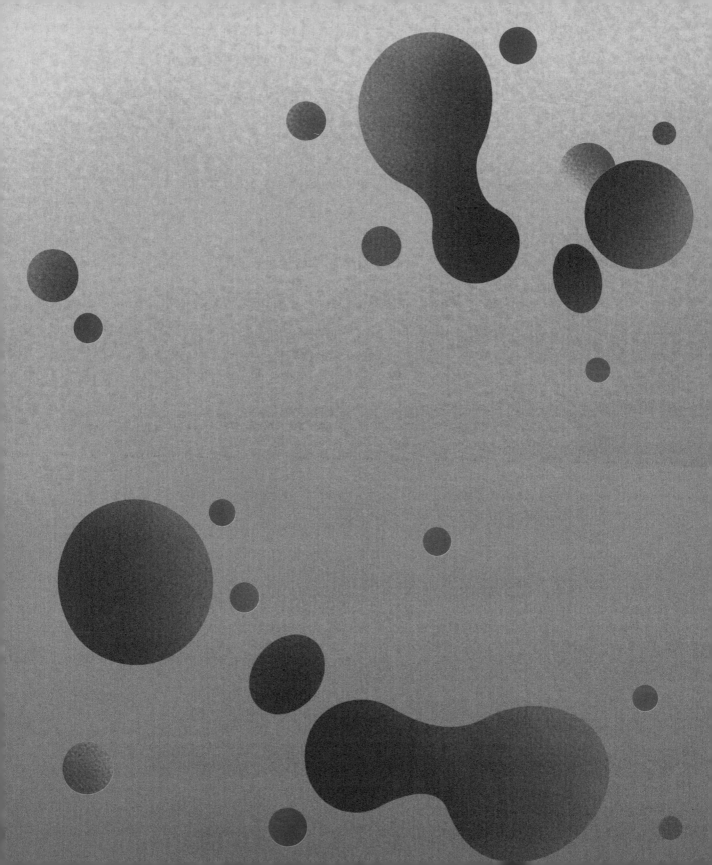